To:

_____

From:

_____

Date:

_____

To the Best Dad in the World

© 2014 Christian Art Gifts, RSA
   Christian Art Gifts Inc., IL, USA

Designed by Christian Art Gifts

Images used under license from Shutterstock.com

Scripture quotations are taken from the *Holy Bible*, New International Version®
NIV®. Copyright © 1973, 1978, 1984, 2011 by International Bible Society. Used by
permission of Zondervan Publishing House. All rights reserved.

Scripture quotations are taken from the *Holy Bible*, New Living Translation®, second
edition. Copyright © 1996, 2004 by Tyndale House Publishers, Inc., Carol Stream,
Illinois 60188. All rights reserved.

Scripture quotations marked ESV are taken from the *Holy Bible*, English Standard
Version, copyright © 2001 by Crossway Bibles, a division of Good News Publishers.
Used by permission. All rights reserved.

Printed in China

ISBN 978-1-4321-0996-7 (Hardcover)
ISBN 978-1-4321-1000-0 (LuxLeather)

Christian Art Gifts has made every effort to trace the ownership of all quotes and
poems in this book. In the event of any question that may arise from the use of any
quote or poem, we regret any error made and will be pleased to make the necessary
correction in future editions of this book.

© All rights reserved. No part of this book may be reproduced in any form without
permission in writing from the publisher, except in the case of brief quotations in
critical articles or reviews.

14 15 16 17 18 19 20 21 22 23 – 10 9 8 7 6 5 4 3 2 1

to the Best No.1 Dad in the world

christian art gifts

Any man can be a father, but it takes someone special to be a dad.

Anonymous

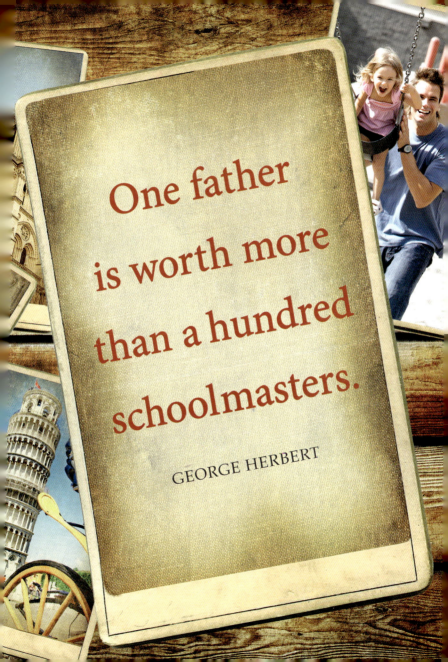

The ultimate measure of a man is not where he stands in moments of comfort and convenience, but where he stands at times of challenge and controversy.

Martin Luther King, Jr.

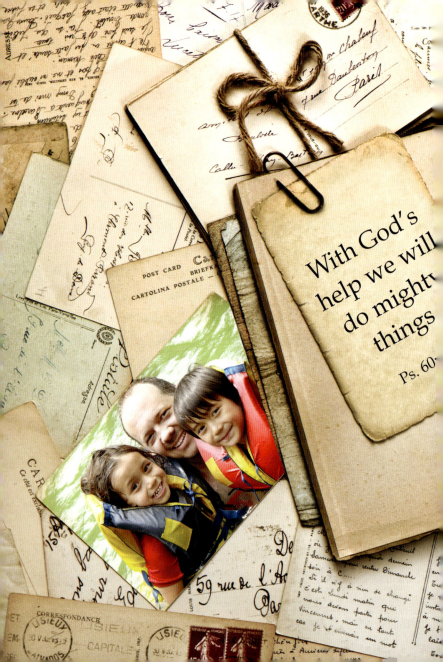

Expect great things from God; attempt great things for God.

WILLIAM CAREY

Let steadfastness have its full effect, that you may be perfect and complete, lacking in nothing.

James 1:4

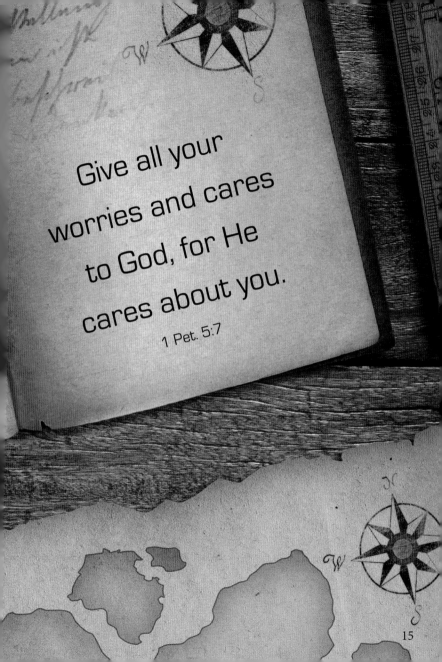

Give all your worries and cares to God, for He cares about you.

1 Pet. 5:7

Never be lacking in zeal, but keep your spiritual fervor, serving the Lord.

Rom. 12:11

The family was ordained by God before He established any other institution, even before He established the church.

Billy Graham

Four steps to achievement:

1. Plan purposefully
2. Prepare prayerfully
3. Proceed positively
4. Pursue persistently

William A. Ward

The Lord is like a father to His children, tender and compassionate.

Ps. 103:13

Children are a gift from the LORD; they are a reward from Him.

Ps. 127:3

We can't form our children
on our own concepts; we must
take them and love them as
God gives them to us.

Johann Wolfgang von Goethe

> Be on guard.
> Stand firm in the faith.
> Be courageous.
> Be strong.
>
> 1 Cor. 16:13

Courage is an inner resolution
to go forward in spite of obstacles
and frightening situations.

Martin Luther King, Jr.

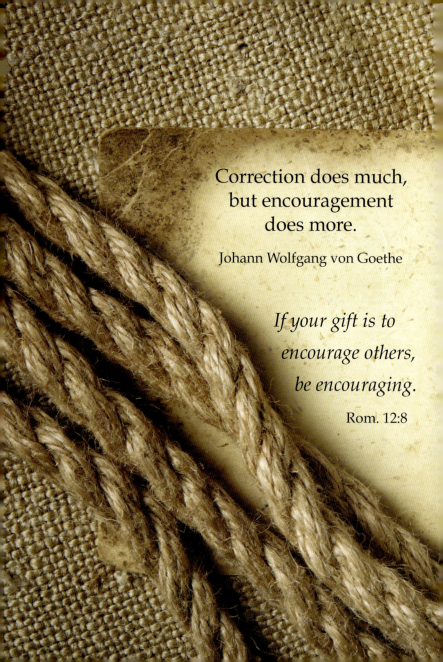

Correction does much,
but encouragement
does more.

Johann Wolfgang von Goethe

*If your gift is to
encourage others,
be encouraging.*

Rom. 12:8

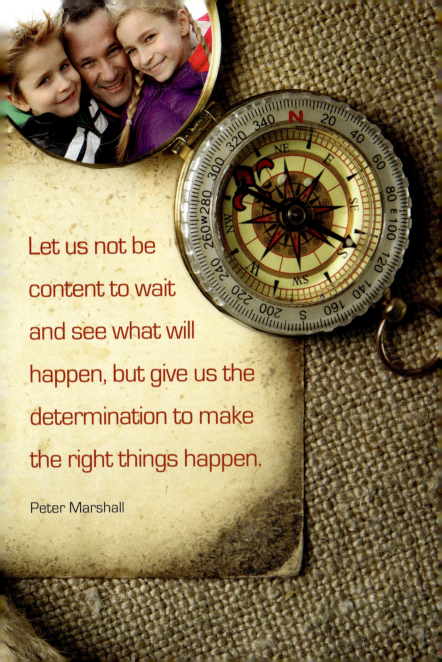

Let us not be content to wait and see what will happen, but give us the determination to make the right things happen.

Peter Marshall

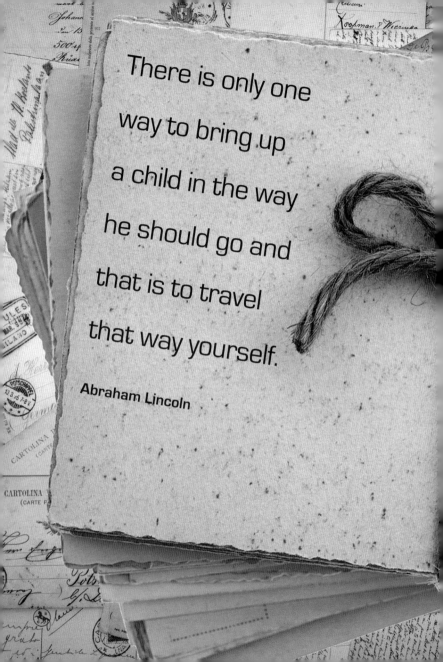

See what kind of love the Father has given to us, that we should be called children of God; and so we are.

1 John 3:1

The first great gift we can bestow on others is a good example.

Thomas Morell

A child is not likely to find a father in God unless he finds something of God in his father.

Austin L. Sorensen

My only aim is to finish the race and complete the task the Lord Jesus has given me – the task of testifying to the good news of God's grace.

Acts 20:24

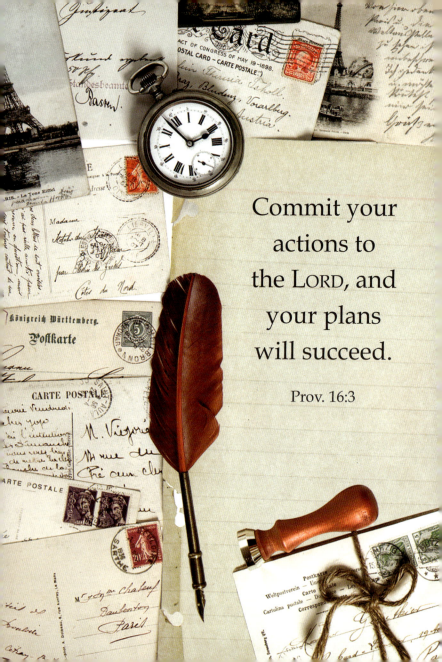

Commit your actions to the LORD, and your plans will succeed.

Prov. 16:3

Aim for a star,
and keep your sights high!
With a heart full of faith within,
your feet on the ground and
your eyes in the sky.

Helen Lowrie Marshall

The best inheritance a parent can give to his children is a few minutes of his time each day.

Orlando A. Battista

In everything set them an example by doing what is good. In your teaching show integrity.

Titus 2:7

No person was ever honored for what he received. Honor has been the reward for what he gave.

Calvin Coolidge

Work hard and become a leader.
Prov. 12:24

Though leadership may be hard to define, the one characteristic common to all leaders is the ability to make things happen.

Ted W. Engstrom

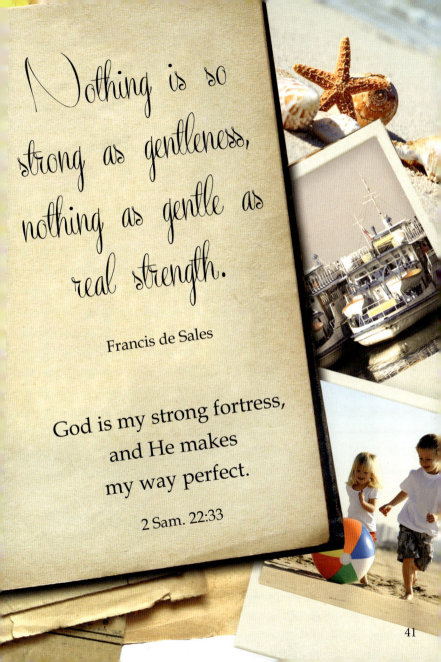

Nothing is so strong as gentleness, nothing as gentle as real strength.

Francis de Sales

God is my strong fortress, and He makes my way perfect.

2 Sam. 22:33

Encourage one another and build one another up.

1 Thess. 5:11

You don't raise heroes,
you raise sons.
And if you treat them like sons,
they'll turn out to be heroes,
even if it's just in your own eyes.

Walter M. Schirra

Giving is the secret of a healthy life. Not necessarily money, but whatever a man has of encouragement and sympathy and understanding.

John D. Rockefeller, Jr.

The father of a righteous child has great joy; a man who fathers a wise son rejoices in him.

Prov. 23:24

You can preach a better sermon with your life than with your lips.

Oliver Goldsmith

A good father is one of the most unsung, unpraised, unnoticed, and yet one of the most valuable assets in our society.

Billy Graham

Take Christ into your heart and the life of your family, and He will transform your home.

Billy Graham